D0585968

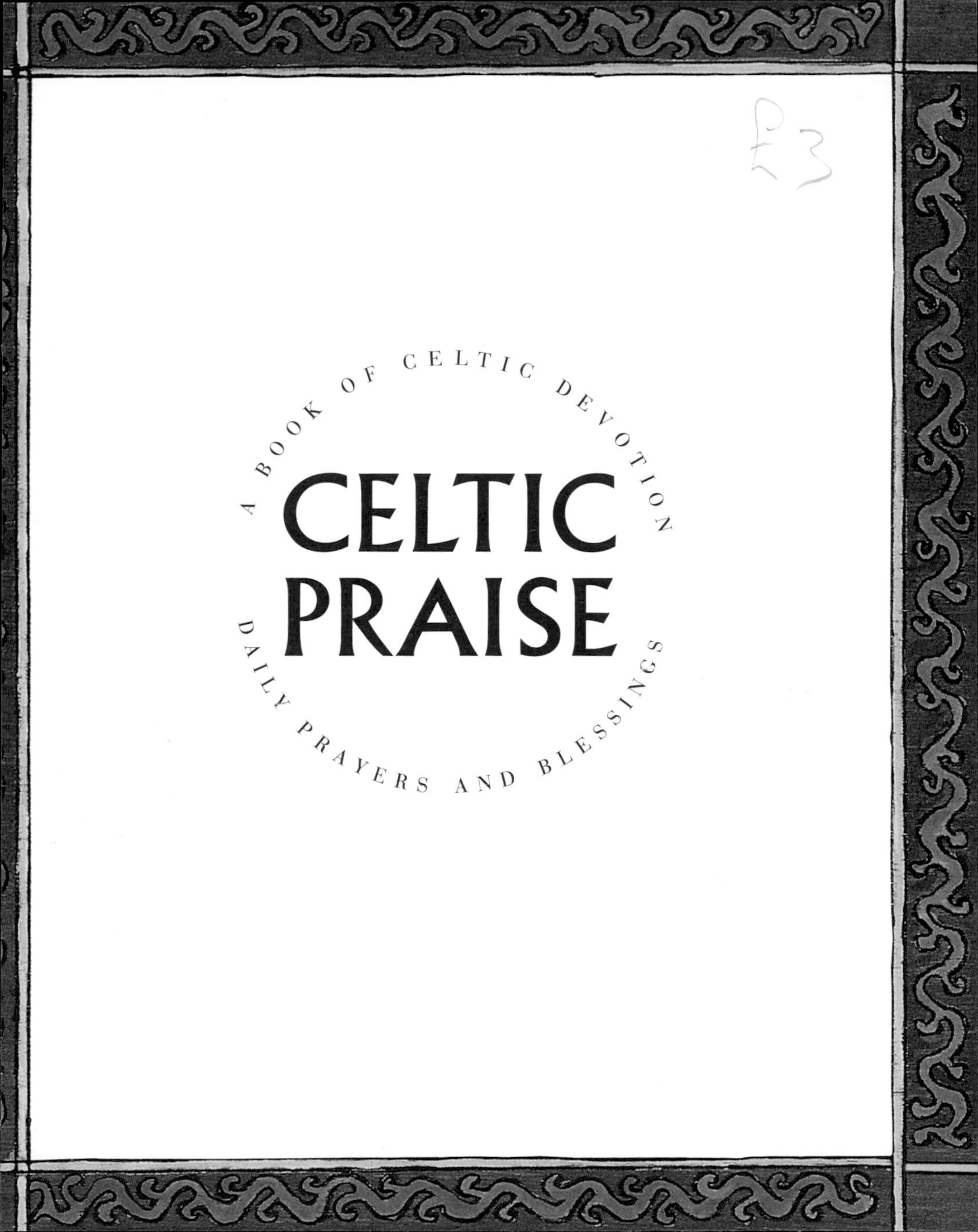
A BOOK OF CELTIC DEVOTION
CELTIC
PRAISE
DAILY PRAYERS AND BLESSINGS

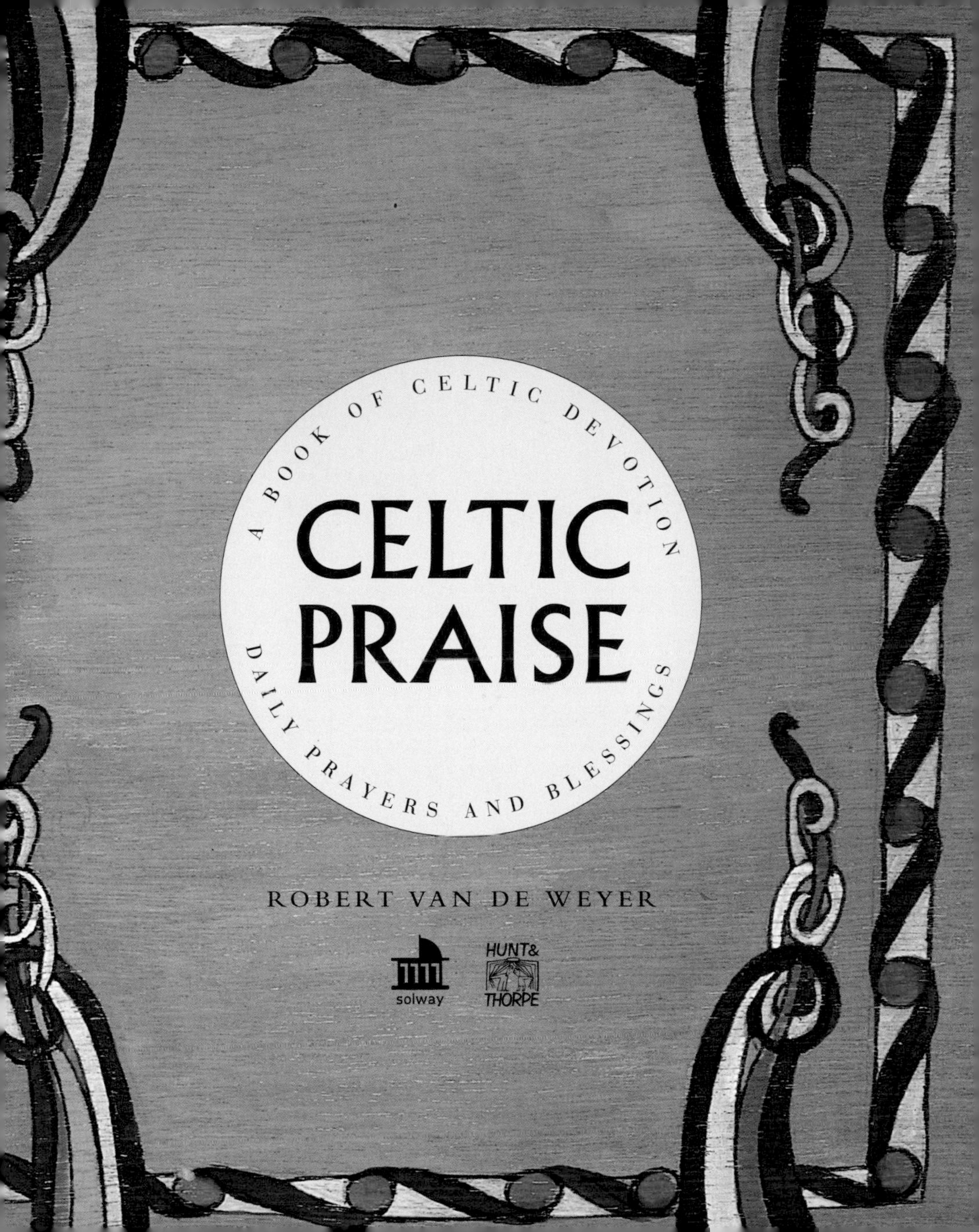
A BOOK OF CELTIC DEVOTION
CELTIC
PRAISE
DAILY PRAYERS AND BLESSINGS
ROBERT VAN DE WEYER
solway
HUNT&
THORPE

ISBN 1-85608-388-8

Designed and produced by
THE BRIDGEWATER BOOK COMPANY LTD.

Write to:
Hunt & Thorpe
Laurel House, Station Approach, New Alresford,
Hampshire, SO24 9JH, UK

Hunt & Thorpe is a name used under licence by
Paternoster Publishing, PO Box 300,
Kingstown Broadway, Carlisle, CA3 0QW, UK

A CIP catalog record for this book is available from the British Library.

Printed and bound in Singapore

THE PRAISES OF THE CELTS

For the Celts, praise was a mixture of gratitude and debate. They constantly thanked God for his many blessings. But they refused to accept these blessings uncritically. Instead they wanted to question why God had acted in a particular way, and what the meaning and intentions of his actions were. They also debated within themselves, questioning whether or not their responses to God's actions were appropriate. To the modern reader the honesty and depth of their spiritual debates can be quite disturbing, and even seem to threaten faith itself. Yet it is precisely because the Celts felt so secure in their faith, that they were able to be so frank with God. In this mixture of gratitude and debate, Celtic praise reflects the Old Testament Psalms. When the Psalmists express thanksgiving, they rise to great poetic heights. Yet they quarrel with God, they doubt his

The security of Celtic faith allowed them to question their God.

wisdom, they vent their anger on him, and they feel at times utterly abandoned by him. Indeed every human emotion, negative and positive, finds a place in the psalms. Although Christians over the past two millennia have continued to recite the psalms, and to acknowledge this on the model of true praise, they have not generally followed the Psalmists' example when composing their own hymns of praise; they have preferred to confine themselves to conventional pious feelings. The Celtic Christians were therefore quite rare and brave in taking their cue from the Psalms. The composers of the Celtic poems and praise contained in this book are unknown. In fact, they probably do not have a single composer. As they were handed down by word of mouth from one generation to the next, some lines were added, and others taken away. And since they were probably sung to a variety of different tunes, the words were altered to fit each new melody. Many poems were undoubtedly lost in the nineteenth century, as the old Celtic languages were replaced by English as the common tongue of Britain and Ireland. But happily a good sample were saved by scholarly collectors traveling to remote villages and farmsteads, and were then translated.

The religious history of Britain and Ireland is often presented as a series of doctrinal and institutional battles. The first was between the native Celtic form of Christianity, and the more sophisticated form imported from Rome. The Roman form is said to have triumphed at the Synod in Whitby. Then, in later centuries the antagonists were Catholics and Protestants. But in truth the Celtic spirit has never been questioned; it has continued to flourish in the popular religion, and in the moral and spiritual attitudes of both islands. The poems of praise brought together in this book reflect and express these attitudes. Some will make orthodox believers raise their eyebrows. Others will induce a degree of emotional discomfort. But in their different ways all will inspire because they all arise from a genuine faith which, like Jacob, wrestles with God.

PART ONE

◆ 1 ◆

GOOD THINGS

"Let the Lord give us what we need
and let heaven stay in heaven."

Heaven on Earth

To the person that sleeps on horsehair
A down mattress is heaven.
To the person that lives on spuds
Roast beef is heaven.
To the person in a rough wool tunic
A silk shirt is heaven.
To the person with a nagging spouse
Quiet solitude is heaven.
To the person living alone
A loving spouse is heaven.
Let the Lord give us what we need,
And let heaven stay in heaven.

The Things of God

You may have a highly polished shoe,
But your footsteps are no grander
Than those made by a barefoot man.
You may have a fine woollen cloak,
But naked your body is no different
From that of a man dressed in rags.
God made the foot, man the shoe.
God made the body, man the cloak.
Cherish the things of God
Above those of man.

Grains of Sand

How many grains of sand on the beach?
How many blades of grass
 in the meadow?
How many drops of dew on the tree?
If you could count all these,
You could count the number
 of God's blessings.
Do not even try to count.
Just trust, and enjoy,
 and give thanks.

"They have watched over my joys and my sorrows."

The Stones of My House

The stones of my house
 are my witnesses.
They have seen all
 my good deeds and bad.
They have watched over
 my joys and my sorrows.
They have observed me
 in every mood.
If they could speak,
 they could tell my story.
Am I glad they are dumb?
Or would I like them to talk?
Am I ashamed or proud of my life?
These stones are the eyes of God.
Whenever I look on those stones,
 let me remember that
 God looks on me.

Wealth as Loan

When I give alms to the poor,
Let me not congratulate myself.
Let there be no pride in my act.
The wealth I possess is on loan;
God has made me its steward.
I am his hands and his heart.
Let my love for others be God's love;
Let my pity for the needy be his;
Let my alms be received as his gift.

"The wealth I possess is on loan;
God has made me its steward."

Home

Where is my home?
Is it the house where I live,
The garden where I sit in summer,
The country where I roam,
Or the church where I worship?
The place I call home
Is where my heart is at rest.
And my heart is most at rest
When it turns to God in prayer.
So wherever I pray is home.

◆ 2 ◆

Good Times

"Don't wait to die, enjoy heaven now;
Don't argue or cavil – just dance."

Heaven Now

If I were in heaven,
I would play my harp,
    and sing songs of praise
    with the angels.
If I were in heaven,
I would dance with joy,
    and fill the air with laughter.
Let earth be like heaven,
    and people like angels;
Let all sing songs of praise.
Don't wait to die,
    enjoy heaven now;
Don't argue or cavil –
    just dance.

Symphony

There is no music so gentle,
No sound so sweet,
No praise so pleasant
As the praise, sound, and music
Of that simple word "Love."
The word itself is like a song,
It conjures images of all that is good.
On the lips it's like a soothing drink.
Let's dance, sing, and play
The symphony of love.

A Meadow in June

I walk through a meadow in June.
Wild flowers stroke my legs,
Red and yellow petals caress me,
The dew on the grass washes me.
Is each tiny flower an angel?
Is each petal an angelic finger?
Are the angels cleansing me of sin?
Are the angels my lovers and friends?
Here and now God is present;
Here and now heaven is on earth;
Here and now eternity is present;
Here and now joy is infinite.

"Are the angels cleansing me of sin?
Are the angels my lovers and friends?"

Welcome Friday

Welcome Friday, I love this day.
The day our Lord was crucified.
A day for quiet reflection,
A day for earnest prayer,
A day to remember one's sins,
A day to beg for forgiveness,
A day to abstain from good food,
A day to shun fine wine,
A day to turn toward goodness,
A day to plan acts of charity,
A day to give thanks for all
God's blessings.

Welcome Sunday

Welcome Sunday, I love this day.
The day our Lord rose to life,
A day of joy and rest,
A day to laugh with family and friends,
A day to play with children,
A day to enjoy the beauty of Nature,
A day to sit at home by the fire,
A day to tell the stories of old,
A day to sing and to dance,
A day to worship the God who made us,
A day to give thanks for all his blessings.

"The day our Lord was crucified"

"A summer morning; my eyes are open."

A Summer Morning

A summer morning;
My eyes are open.
The sun is bright:
I see clouds scudding by,
Birds in the air,
Flowers in the meadow,
Bees in the flowers,
Cows eating grass.
A summer morning;
My eyes are closed.
The sun is warm:
I hear birds singing,
Bees buzzing,
Cows munching
I feel wind on my cheek,
Smell flowers beneath me.
All my senses are alive.
Thank God for beauty.

"All my senses are alive.
Thank God for beauty."

PART TWO

◆ 3 ◆

GOOD FAMILIES

"Instead I shall turn to God for counsel,
And I shall beg him to guide my actions."

Good Advice

My father gave me good advice.
I heard what he said,
but did not listen to his words.
My father gave me many blessings.
But I was indifferent to both
his blessings and his curses.
Now my father has died,
and I have lost him.
I am old enough to listen,
but he no longer speaks.
I want him to bless me,
but his hand is cold and limp.
I can never get him back.
Instead I shall turn to God for
counsel, and I shall beg him
to guide my actions.
Goodbye father; welcome Father.

Test of Brotherhood

People have always argued and disagreed.
On every matter there have been two sides.
Christ urged us to love and be united.
On every matter he wanted perfect harmony.
Christians have continued to argue
and disagree.
On matters of doctrine there have
been two sides.
Can we argue and remain united?
Can we disagree and remain in harmony?
That is the true test of brotherhood.

"Can we disagree and remain in harmony? This is the true test of brotherhood."

Man and Woman

If God has made us all to love one another,
Is it not true that any man
can love any woman,
And that any woman can love any man?
Husband, why be discontent
with your wife?
Wife, why be discontent
with your husband?
Whoever you are,
God has made you for love.
There is no such thing as a bad marriage.
Any marriage, between any man
and any woman,
Can be good if God is the master.

"Whoever you are,
God has made you for love."

Free Kisses

A wedding is a costly business.
Money is needed for the priest
and his clerk.
Money is needed for the hire
of the church.
Money is needed to feed the guests.
Money is needed for robes to wear.
Love by contrast is entirely free.
Free are the smiles that play
on the lips;
Free are the kisses stolen
by moonlight;
Free are the words whispered
at midnight;
Free are the strolls hand in hand
through the wood.
We are rich in love but poor in money.
The priests say our union is sinful.
May God, who blesses us, forgive.

"We are rich in love but poor in money."

"I long to be as close to God
As I am to her – and closer still."

Married to God

As I lie in bed with my wife
I can sense the warmth of her body;
I can hear the steady rhythm
of her breath;
I can touch her soft, smooth skin;
I can smell the sweetness of her body;
I can see the silhouette of her figure.
I love her as I love myself.
Do I love God as I love my wife?
Do I love Christ as I love myself?
Is God in Christ as near me as she?
Can I sense, hear, touch, smell,
and see him
As I sense, hear, touch, smell,
and see her?
I long to be as close to God
As I am to her - and closer still.

"Do I love Christ as I love myself?"

◆ 4 ◆

Good Friends

*"He was weak and he was foolish.
In this lay his strength and wisdom."*

True Strength

If Christ and the largest man
in the world
were locked in combat;
And Christ were to knock
the largest man
onto the muddy turf;
Would that convince you that
Christ is truly strong?
If Christ and the cleverest man
in the world
were locked in debate;
And Christ were to
outwit the cleverest man
in verbal battle;
Would that convince you that
Christ is truly wise?
Yet Christ told us to turn
the other cheek;
And he allowed himself
to be killed by cleverer men.
He was weak and he was foolish.
In this lay his strength and wisdom.

Being Dependent

When Jesus came to earth as a baby,
He depended entirely on human love -
That of Mary, Joseph, and the shepherds.
When Jesus preached and healed,
He depended entirely on human love -
The alms given by those who heard him.
I too depend on human love.
The kindness of others sustains my soul.
The gifts of others sustain my body.
Every person depends on others' love.
Let no one be ashamed of their needs.
To depend on others is to imitate Christ.

Friends of Sadness

When I am happy,
I have many friends.
I am witty in conversation,
making people laugh.
I sing sweet ballads,
making people cry.
So they are glad
of my company.
When I am sad,
I have few friends.
I become dull of mind,
with nothing to say.
I become dull of heart,
with no will to sing.
So people shun my company.
The friends of sadness
are true friends.

Kneading and Rising

As I knead the flour
I think of all the many grains
That have been ground to make it.
Christ's church is like flour
Made up of many people of many races
Ground up to make a single dough.
As I watch the dough rise
I think of the yeast's power
Raising up the weight of flour and water.
Prayer in Christ is like rising dough
Drawing together every hope and fear
And lifting them up to God.

THE BLESSINGS OF KINDNESS

May those who oppress
the poor be cursed.
May no butter crown their milk;
May their ducks yield no down;
May fire in summer burn their crops;
May midges eat their flesh.
May those who feed
the poor be blessed.
May their milk be thick with cream;
May they sleep on softest pillows;
May their crops be heavy with grain;
May they always be hale and strong.

MY ENEMIES

From the enemies of my land,
From the enemies of my faith,
From the enemies of
all that is good and true,
May the cross of Christ preserve me.
May the cross bring us peace,
May the cross bring us love,
May the cross preserve us
from all evil and lies,
And carry us to the safety of heaven.

"May the cross preserve us from all evil and lies..."

"Open your heart to Christ, and he will enter."

Enemies into Friends

It is better to roam the world
With a stick in your hand
For pulling fruit from trees,
Than a sword at your side
For killing enemies.
God has put fruit on trees
To sustain our bodies,
And love in our hearts
To make enemies into friends.

Friendship with Christ

A person who approaches Christ
with flattery makes no impression.
One who pretends to moral virtue
is seen for what he is.
A person who takes pride in religious
observance is not respected.
One who demands friendship
is gently spurned.
Friendship with Christ cannot
be claimed, but only received.
It is not a right, but privilege.
Open your heart to Christ,
and he will enter.
Come to him on your knees,
and he will raise you up.

PART THREE

◆ 5 ◆

Good Thoughts

"I thought I was serving God.
In truth I was serving pride."

Fame

Long ago I was famous.
People called me golden-tongued.
They flocked to hear me preach.
I was the finest speaker in the land.
But fame withers faster than wealth.
I lost my skill at speaking.
I lost my desire to inspire.
Soon the people forgot me.
I thought I was serving God.
In truth I was serving pride.
I thought myself full of joy.
In truth my soul was rotten.
Thank God for taking fame away.
Thank God for giving humility.

Striving for Success

When I was striving for success,
To make my mark upon the world,
I committed many sins,
I exploited many people
In order to achieve my purposes.
When my conscience pricked, I said:
All will be justified when
my task is done.
Now that I have finished striving,
And no longer want to
make more marks,
I want only to be pure,
and live in harmony with the world.
I see no difference between
action and purpose;
The action is the purpose,
The purpose the action.
All must be justified here and now.

Reasons for Trembling

There are four reasons
why a person may tremble.
The person may be frightened,
and tremble with fear.
The person may be ill,
and tremble with a fever.
The person may be angry,
and tremble with rage.
The person may be in love,
and tremble with passion.
Fear, fever, rage, passion –
All are created by God.
What makes us frightened,
What makes us ill,
What makes us angry,
What makes us love –
On these matters
we have some choice,
On these we must
seek God's grace.

The World and the Church

In the world people
get what they pay for.
So the rich,
who have much to spend,
have much to enjoy;
While the poor,
who have little to spend,
have little to enjoy.
In church they should
get what they need.
So the rich,
who at present have much,
should give much and receive little;
While the poor,
who at present have little,
should give little, and receive much.
Let the world flourish
and prosper;
And the church
set right its wrongs.

"Let the world flourish and prosper;
And the church set right its wrongs."

"Will I continue to love and trust him
Even in this bleak, harsh wilderness?"

No Grass Grows

I roam where no grass will grow.
The bees make no honey,
The cows are dry.
At night the moon withholds
her borrowed light;
By day the sun is shrouded
in dark clouds.
The wheat and barley wither
on the stalk,
Fruits shrivel before they ripen.
God has withdrawn his blessings.
He has decided to test my faith.
Will I continue to love and trust him
Even in this bleak, harsh wilderness?
He does not bless me,
I want to curse him.
Let my curses melt into blessings.

"A person's good work may be remembered
Long after his body has rotted."

Good News

Fame may outlast a person's life;
A person's good work
  may be remembered
  long after his body has rotted.
Verses from a poet's pen
  may outlast the name of the poet,
  as the poems are sung and repeated.
Lasting longer than fame or verses
  is the book that speaks
  with undying tongue.
Good news of Christ lasts for ever.

◆ 6 ◆

GOOD FAITH

"The Lord alone can set me free.
In him alone can I put my trust."

Lifting the Burden

Throughout my life
I have never confessed my sins.
I have never apologized
to people I hurt.
I have never sought to make amends.
I have assumed time would
blot out my wrongs.
But now I am old and close to death.
The sins of my past lie heavy
on my soul.
I can still recall the wrongs
I have done.
Time has not blotted them out.
To confess now would
cost me nothing.
Those whom I hurt are old or dead.
There is nothing I could do
to make amends.
How can this burden be lifted?
The Lord alone can set me free.
In him alone can I put my trust.

Complex Doctrines

I am full of doubt; yet I trust in God.
I cannot believe all I am taught.
The doctrines of the church are complex.
Some I cannot understand.
Some seem to make no sense.
Some make sense, but are implausible.
The priest may tell me I'm a sinner;
He may inform me that good people believe
– That doubt is a sign of sin.
Yet I trust in God.
His love makes sense.
His love is confirmed by his blessings.

"I am full of doubt;
yet I trust in God."

Low, High, and Deep Prayers

I send low prayers along the ground.
These are for Jesus Christ;
Asking him to heal all people.
I send high prayers into the sky.
These are for our Father in heaven,
Asking him to bring peace to the world.
I send deep prayers into my heart.
These are for the Holy Spirit
Asking him to heal and pacify my heart.

"Ask him to heal
and pacify my heart."

Thanking God

I thank God for this horse-hair mattress.
I thank him for this down-filled pillow,
And also for this warm, wool blanket.
I thank God for the gift of sleep.
I thank him for peace of mind,
And also for soothing my limbs.
I thank God for the nights awake.
I thank him when my mind keeps turning,
And also for a restless body.
The nights of sleep are a joy.
The nights awake are a trial.
Through both my faith is deepened.

"So I shall utter the words, and let the Spirit do the rest."

Praying with Spirit

Sometimes when I pray,
I utter the words,
but I do not feel or think them.
Sometimes when I pray,
I utter the words,
thinking about what I say,
but not feeling.
Sometimes when I pray,
I utter the words,
and I both think and feel
what I say.
An act of will cannot
make me feel,
nor stop my mind
From wandering.
An act of will can only
make me utter.
So I shall utter the words,
and let the Spirit do the rest,
guiding my mind and heart
as he wills.

"Salvation is its harvest."

God's Law

Where are God's laws?
Are they found in a book?
Is the gospel a book of law?
What are God's laws?
Are they a set of rules?
Is salvation blind obedience?
God's law is in our hearts.
It is our desire for goodness.
The gospel helps that desire to grow.
Salvation is its harvest.

"The war against sin gives life its zest."

A Soldier to His General

When I come to God to
confess my sins,
Do I need to lie face down
on the ground?
Should I grovel and abase
myself before him?
He allowed sin and evil into this world;
He gave me freedom to choose
good or bad;
He put selfish desires in my breast.
The challenge of sin
is the purpose of life;
The war against sin gives life its zest.
Without evil I could not
know goodness.
I come to God as a soldier
to his general;
I ask him for stronger weapons
in battle,
He inspires me to fight -
My head is held high.

PART FOUR

◆ 7 ◆

GOOD LIVING

"Praise him for what I enjoy.
Smile at what I lack."

The Glad Beggar

Let those with well-paid jobs
Merchants, lawyers, and the like
Be grateful for their wealth.
Let those with food on the table,
And a roof above their heads,
Rejoice in their security.
But I am glad to be a beggar.
One day I go hungry and cold,
The next I have food and warmth.
I have learnt never to be bitter,
Even when my luck is down;
And to praise God when luck is up.
Praise him for what I enjoy.
Smile at what I lack.

Never Mock

Never mock what others say.
Perhaps their words are full of nonsense.
Perhaps they are trying to puff themselves up.
Perhaps they like hearing the sound
of their voices.
Perhaps they are trying to deceive their hearers.
Perhaps they are foolish and dim.
Perhaps they more clever than wise.
Yet amidst the useless clay.
You may find jewels beyond price.
The word of God is in every heart,
And can speak through every voice.

Protection on a Journey

When I set out on a journey,
I offer seven prayers.
I pray that God will protect me
From falling into a river and drowning,
From getting lost and dying of cold,
From being attacked and
beaten by robbers,
From gambling and losing my money,
From contracting a terrible fever,
From being tempted by sexual favors,
From making friends with evil people.
I am too stupid and too weak
to protect myself.
God alone can guard me,
And bring me safely back home.

*"God alone can guard me,
And bring me safely back home."*

Rising in the Morning

*When you rise in the morning,
what fills your head?
Are you thinking of
food and drink,
the pleasures ahead?
Are you planning
the work you must do,
the labor ahead?
Are you fearful of
snares and dangers,
the evils ahead?
Are you hopeful of
all you'll achieve,
the successes ahead?
Let all those worldly thoughts
swirl in your mind;
Then let them flush away,
like dirt in a river.
Empty your head;
Let your brain be at peace.
Quietly, calmly, serenely
Offer the day to God.*

"Quietly, calmly, serenely offer the day to God."

Controling the Heart

The priests tell me
that if I sin with
my will and inclination,
it is as if the deed is done.
My conscience tells me
that if I want to sin,
yet restrain myself,
God will bless me for my virtue.
Does sin lie in the heart or in action?
Minute by minute I can control my actions.
It takes a lifetime and more
to control the heart.

A Bad Back

From years of digging and lifting,
From years of plowing and sowing,
From years of reaping and threshing,
My back is in permanent pain.
At night when the pain prevents slumber
I curse those years of toil.
In daylight when the pain prevents work,
I pray to God for strength.
In those few moments
when the pain eases,
My joy in life is immense
– praise God.
After those moments when the pain
returns I long for heaven's joy
– praise God.

Am I a Burden?

Am I a burden, now I am old?
My deaf ears force you to shout.
My wobbly legs force you to clean for me.
My bent fingers force you to sew for me.
My twisted back forces you to dress me.
My fading eyes force you to lead me.
My toothless mouth forces you
to make soup for me.
Will you be pleased when I die?
Yet you tell me you love me.
You enjoy listening to my stories.
You ask me my advice.
You make me feel important.
I still need to be needed
And you express your mind.
If you are deceiving me,
God bless you for your deception.

Passing Time

To a child a few weeks seem long.
To a youth a few months seem long.
To an adult a few years seem long.
To an old person decades seem short.
The old person is closest to God.
To God decades are seconds,
Centuries minutes.
To him eternity is every moment.
Be patient with yourself;
Think like God.

"Be patient with yourself;
think like God."

◆ 8 ◆

Good Dying

"And there is God
Wanting me to come back home."

Sudden Death

Let me not die suddenly.
I want to be warned of
    my impending death.
I need time to order
    my material affairs,
And time to confess
    my sins and repent.
But surely I could always keep
    my affairs in order.
Surely I could confess
    my sins as soon as I commit them.
Then I would be ready
    whenever God wanted me.
I would be happy to die suddenly.

Who are Waiting?

Who are waiting for me to die?
Who are watching my failing body?
There is the devil
    wanting to entice my soul to hell.
There are my children
    wanting to inherit my land and gold.
There is the worm
    wanting to eat my rotting flesh.
And there is God
    wanting me to come back home.

Stretching Out

I stretch myself out on this bed
As in the coffin I shall be stretched.
I ask God to give me sweet dreams,
As in death I shall ask to enter heaven.
I look forward to rising again
in the morning,
As after death I look forward
to rising with Christ.
Let me rest as peacefully as
I shall rest in my coffin;
May my dreams carry me
to heavenly joy;
May I rise with fresh vigor
to walk with Christ.

God's Flock

When you go out on the hills
To tend your flock,
You ask yourself daily:
Have any gone astray?
So you count your sheep one by one;
And if any are missing,
You start to search.
We are God's flock,
And the hills are his world.
He asks himself daily:
Have any gone astray?
So he counts his sheep one by one;
And if any are missing, he starts to search.
When winter comes,
You round up your sheep,
And you and your dogs
Lead them to shelter.
It's too late to search.
The wandering sheep die on the hills.
When death comes,
God rounds up his sheep,
And he and his angels lead them to heaven.
It's then too late to search.
The wandering sheep die in hell.
We know when winter is coming,
But death may come at any time.
So do not wander from God's flock,
Lest you're away when the searching stops.

*"I trust in God;
may he protect me from all danger."*

Lying Down with God

I lie down with God;
May he lie down with me.
I sleep with God;
May he be present in my dreams.
I trust in God;
May he protect me from all danger.
I rise up with God;
May God rise up with me.
I walk with God;
May he always be at my side.
I rely on God;
May he strengthen me in my labor.
I eat with God;
May God be in my bread.
I drink with God;
May God be in my wine.
I live with God;
May God live within me.

*"When they bury my body deep within the boggy peat,
may my soul continue to glow."*

Sparing the Fire

Each night I spare the fire,
My last act before retiring.
I bury two fresh lumps of peat
Deep within the embers.
Then tomorrow when I wake
I can poke the fire to life.
At death may God spare me.
When they bury my body
Deep within the boggy peat,
May my soul continue to glow.
So when the last trumpet sounds
I can rise with Christ to life.

Reason Growing Dim

Does your reason now grow dim?
Do you now find it hard
to think clearly?
Does logic seem like a hammer
in your head,
Battering your soft brain into a pulp?
Perhaps age is weakening your mind.
Perhaps your reason is fading
with the years.
Or perhaps you have seen
the limits of logic,
And recognized how
little logic can discern.
Whether age or wisdom is the cause,
Welcome the confusion
of your thoughts.
Out of chaos God created the world.
Out of confusion truth appears.

BIBLIOGRAPHY

This is a list of primary sources concerning Celtic Christianity.

Anderson, A.O. and M.O., *Adomnan's Life of St. Columba*, London, 1961.

Bieler, L., *The Patrician Texts in the Book of Armagh*, Dublin, 1979.

Carmichael, A., *Carmina Gadelica*, 2 vols, Edinburgh, 1928.

Clough, S.D.P., *A Gaelic Anthology*, Dublin, 1987.

Colgrave, R., *Two Lives of St. Cuthbert*, Cambridge, 1940.

Doble, G.H., *Lives of the Welsh Saints*, Cardiff, 1971.

Flower, R.E.W., *Poems and Translations*, London, 1931.

Forbes, A.P., *Lives of St. Ninian and St. Kentigern*, Edinburgh, 1874.

Graves, A.P., *A Celtic Psaltery*, London, 1917.

Greene, D. and O'Connor, F., *A Golden Treasury of Irish Poetry 600 to 1200* AD, London, 1967.

Hull, E., *The Poem-Book of the Gael*, London, 1912.

Hyde, D., *The Religious Songs of Connacht*, 2 vols, Dublin, 1906.

Jackson, K., *Studies in Early Celtic Poetry*, Cambridge, 1935.

McLean, G.R.D., *Poems of the Western Highlanders*, London, 1961.

Metcalfe, W.M., *Lives of Scottish Saints*, 2 vols, Paisley, 1899.

Meyer, K., *Selections from Ancient Irish Poetry*, London, 1911.

Murphy, G., *Early Irish Lyrics*, Oxford, 1956.

O'Donoghue, D., *St. Brendan the Voyager*, Dublin, 1895.

Rees, W.J., *Lives of the Cambro British Saints*, Llandovery, 1853.

Sharp, E., *Lyra Celtica*, Edinburgh, 1896.

Stevens, J., *Bede's Ecclesiastical History of the English Nation*, London, 1910.

Stokes, W., *Lives of Saints from the Book of Lismore*, Oxford, 1890.

Webb, J.F., *Lives of the Saints*, London, 1965.